Set Yourself Free Little Children and Come to Me

Little Sparrow Ministries

Copyright © 2001 2003 2009, 2017
Little Sparrow Ministries
All Rights Reserved
Printed in the United States of America
International Standard Book Number:
978-1-4276-1692-2

Little Sparrow Ministries
PO Box 307
Lindale, Texas 75771

E-mail: lsparrowministries@gmail.com
Web site:
www.littlesparrowministries.com

No part of this book may be reproduced or transmitted in any form or by any means, electronic or mechanical, including photocopying, recording, or by any information storage and retrieval system, without permission in writing from Little Sparrow Ministries.

Scripture quotations are taken from the *HOLY BIBLE, NEW INTERNATIONAL VERSIONÒ NIV.* Copyright © 1973, 1978, 1984 by International Bible Society. Used by permission of Zondervan. All rights reserved.

**INGRAM BOOK COMPANY
DISTRIBUTORS**

INTRODUCTION

We strongly suggest that parents work with their children while they are reading this book. **PLEASE PRAY EVERY PRAYER OUT LOUD.**

There are two deliverance books for your children. As to which one to use, it depends upon several considerations: age, behavior, and their natural and spiritual conditions.

The other deliverance book is titled, ***Truths vs. Lies, Deliverance for Teenagers.***

In severe cases, the parents can command the spirits to leave while their children are sleeping. We also recommend that the parents go through the adult deliverance book before working with their children.

If you need counsel or advice, please contact me at lsparrowministries@gmail.com.

God bless.

Judy H Farris-Smith

My Child,

If you desire to walk closer with me and have more understanding of my purposes for your life, then experience my love through these pages.

Open your heart to me.

I love you,

God

TABLE OF CONTENTS

Prayer of Salvation 1
I believe... 2
Beginning Prayer 3
Strongmen.. 4
Truth... 5
Forgiveness 6
Putting God First.................................... 7
Activities that are Harmful to Me............ 8
Fortune Teller and Magic 9
Angry, Lies, Gossip, and Pride.............. 10
Sadness, Sorrow, and Loneliness 11
Evil Actions 12
Sickness and Disease 13
Fear, Worry, and Stress 14
Does Not Believe in Jesus 15
Death.. 16
Rebellion vs Submission 17
Releasing Soul-Ties 18
Victory 19
The Keys to Obedience........................ 20
Opening the Doors............................... 21
Armor of God 22
Prayer of Agreement............................ 23
Water Baptism 24
Holy Spirit Baptism 25

Spiritually Clean your Room 27
Clothing with Occult Signs and
Symbols 28
Jewelry with Occult Signs and
Symbols 30
Memory Verses 32
Glossary 33
Keeping your Children Spiritually
Safe 35
Reference Books 37
Other Books by Little Sparrow 38

PRAYER OF SALVATION

If you have not asked our Lord Jesus Christ into your heart, please do so now. He is waiting to take you into his light.

"Jesus, forgive my sins. I confess you to be the Christ, the Son of the living God, and I receive you as my Lord and Savior.

Thank you for washing my sins away with your blood and for giving me the gift of your Holy Spirit. Amen."

I BELIEVE

I BELIEVE God is my heavenly Father and Jesus is his Son.

I BELIEVE that the Holy Spirit is my friend on earth who comforts and guides me and keeps me on God's path for my life.

I BELIEVE God speaks Truth to me through the Bible that was written by God.

I BELIEVE that Jesus loves me so much that he died for me and arose again.

I BELIEVE through Jesus Christ I can do all things. Jesus is my strength when I am weak.

I BELIEVE that He has given me spiritual authority over the enemy's plans and schemes.

I BELIEVE I should obey the Ten Commandments that God gave us, but most of all, love the Lord my God with all my heart.

BEGINNING PRAYER

Dear Lord,

Have mercy on me. I am seeking you for complete freedom. Lord, I want to be closer to you.

Now with the authority given to me by my Lord Jesus Christ, I speak to anything not of God to be bound to silence that is in or around me. In the name of Jesus, you cannot inflict any pain, speak to my mind, or prevent me from hearing, seeing, or speaking. Amen.

 As God's children we are always dealing with forces of darkness. Jesus called them evil spirits and strongmen.

Even though we cannot see them, the enemy is here. But God is with us always so we should never be afraid. *"For God did not give us a spirit of timidity (fear), but a spirit of power, of love, and of self-discipline (a sound mind)."* 2 Timothy 1:7

Remember: *"You dear children, are from God and have overcome them, because the one (God) who is in you is greater than the one (Satan) who is in the world."* 1 John 4:4

The following prayers are for you to speak out loud. The enemy must hear you. They cannot read your mind. *"I have given you authority to trample on snakes and scorpions and to overcome all the power of the enemy; nothing will harm you."* Luke 10:19

TRUTH

When Jesus was a little boy, he went to the Temple without telling his parents. His parents were angry because they could not find him for three days.

He told them the Truth that he was in the Temple, his heavenly Father's house. Always speak Truth as Jesus did.

In the name of Jesus, I bind and cast out of me the strongman of lying spirits, and I loosen Truth and the Holy Spirit into my life.

Lord, help me always to speak the truth. Amen.

FORGIVENESS

When Joseph was a young boy, his brothers sold him into slavery. Joseph later forgave them.

Lord, I forgive anyone that has hurt me or has caused me pain.

Lord, forgive me if I have hurt anyone or caused him or her pain. (Do you need to go to someone and ask for forgiveness?)

Please, Lord, forgive both of us.

Holy Spirit help me to have a forgiving heart. Amen.

PUTTING GOD FIRST

God gave Moses the Ten Commandments. The Ten Commandments are rules to obey. Exodus 20:1-17

The first and greatest commandment is:

"Love the Lord your God with all your heart and with all your soul and with all your mind." Matthew 22:37-38

Lord, help me to put you first in my life and not my own wants or needs. Lord, forgive me if I have not put you first. Amen.

ACTIVITIES THAT ARE HARMFUL TO ME

Ouija board, good luck charms, crystal balls, Dungeons and Dragons, martial arts, Pokeman, Masters of the Universe, ungodly music and literature such as Harry Potter books, blood pacts, magic, Astrology, horoscopes, Yoga, palm reading, tattoos, Rainbow and Demolay organizations, religious organizations that do not declare Jesus Christ as Lord and Savior, smoking, drugs, alcohol, and witchcraft. These are just a few of the harmful and ungodly activities.

Lord, please forgive me for any harmful activities that I have been involved with, those that I know of and do not know of. (Name the activities.)

FORTUNE TELLER AND MAGIC

Lord, I ask you to forgive me for my sins.

In the name of Jesus, I bind and cast out of me the strongmen of divination and familiar spirits according to Matthew 18:18. You are now bound, and I send you to the arid places never to return.

In the name of Jesus, I ask you to separate me from all generational curses/sins as a result of the strongmen of divination and familiar spirits. I shut the open blood line doors to these curses. Holy Spirit fill me with your presence.

I invite the Holy Spirit to guide me each and every day. Amen.

ANGER, LIES, GOSSIP, AND PRIDE

Lord, I ask you to forgive me for my sins.

In the name of Jesus, I bind and cast out of me the strongmen of jealousy, lying spirits, pride, and seducing spirits according to Matthew 18:18. You are now bound, and I send you to the arid places never to return.

In the name of Jesus, I ask you to separate me from all generational curses/sins as a result of the strongmen of jealousy, lying spirits, pride, and seducing spirits. I shut the open blood line doors to these curses. Holy Spirit fill me with your presence.

Lord, I ask to be humble like you and to have your wisdom. Amen.

SADNESS, SORROW, AND LONELINESS

Lord, I ask you to forgive me for my sins.

In the name of Jesus, I bind and cast out of me the strongmen of heaviness and the dumb and deaf spirit according to Matthew 18:18. You are now bound, and I send you to the arid places never to return.

In the name of Jesus, I ask you to separate me from all generational curses/sins as a result of the strongmen of heaviness and the dumb and deaf spirit. I shut the open blood line doors to these curses. Holy Spirit fill me with your presence.

Lord, I ask that you give me your joy and peace in everything I do. Amen.

EVIL ACTIONS

Lord, I ask you to forgive me for my sins.

In the name of Jesus, I bind and cast out of me the strongmen of perverse spirit and whoredoms according to Matthew 18:18. You are now bound, and I send you to the arid places never to return.

In the name of Jesus, I ask you to separate me from all generational curses/sins as a result of the strongmen of perversion. I shut the open blood line doors to these curses. Holy Spirit fill me with your presence.

Lord, I ask that you give me a pure heart and mind Amen.

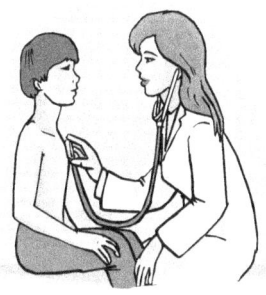

SICKNESS AND DISEASE

Lord, I ask you to forgive me for my sins.

In the name of Jesus, I bind and cast out of me the strongman of infirmity according to Matthew 18:18. You are now bound, and I send you to the arid places never to return.

In the name of Jesus, I ask you to separate me from all generational curses/sins as a result of the strongman of infirmity. I shut the open blood line doors to these curses. Holy Spirit fill me with your presence.

Lord, I ask that you heal me of all sicknesses and diseases. You say in the Bible that if I would cry out to you for help that you would restore my health. I am crying out to you. Amen.

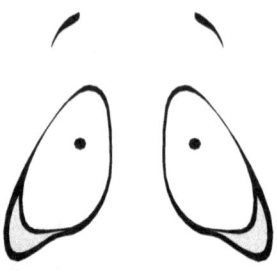

FEAR, WORRY, AND STRESS

Lord, I ask you to forgive me for my sins.

In the name of Jesus, I bind and cast out of me the strongmen of bondage and fear according to Matthew 18:18. You are now bound, and I send you to the arid places never to return.

In the name of Jesus, I ask you to separate me from all generational curses/sins as a result of the strongmen of bondage and fear. I shut the open blood line doors to these curses. Holy Spirit fill me with your presence.

Lord, I ask that you increase my trust in you, and give me your strength to face each day. Amen.

DOES NOT BELIEVE IN JESUS

Lord, I ask you to forgive me for my sins.

In the name of Jesus, I bind and cast out of me the strongmen of the spirit of anti-Christ and spirit of error as it says in Matthews 18:18. You are now bound, and I send you to the arid places never to return.

In the name of Jesus, I ask you to separate me from all generational curses/sins as a result of the strongmen of the spirit of anti-Christ and spirit of error. I shut the open blood line doors to these curses. Holy Spirit fill me with your presence.

Lord, draw me closer to you and give me the desire to read your word. Amen

DEATH

Lord, I ask you to forgive me for my sins.

In the name of Jesus, I bind and cast out of me the strongman of death according to Matthew 18:18. You are now bound, and I send you to the arid places never to return. Holy Spirit come and fill me with your presence.

In the name of Jesus, I ask you to separate me from all generational curses/sins as a result of the strongman of death. I shut the open blood line doors to these curses.

Lord, I thank you for giving me life and victory over death and darkness. Amen.

REBELLION VS SUBMISSION

Lord, I know that in action and attitude I have sinned against you with a rebellious heart. I ask your forgiveness for my rebellion, and I ask that you will shed light on all my evil ways so that I may know the full extent of my rebelliousness.

I bind the spirit of rebellion and cast it out of me. I loosen a submissive spirit and a servant's heart. Holy Spirit please come and fill me with your presence. Amen.

RELEASING SOUL-TIES

If a parent, family member, or perhaps a close friend has died, your child is probably going through the different stages of grief. However, releasing the soul-tie with the deceased person can make their life easier. Just have the child pray the following short prayer:

In the name of Jesus, I break the soul-tie with _____ (name).

I also ask you, Lord, to heal my emotions and to assemble and heal all the fragmented pieces of my soul.

I decree that my soul has been restored. I plead the blood of Christ over my body, soul, and spirit. Amen.

VICTORY

Our heavenly Father says the greatest commandment is for you:

"... to love the Lord your God, to walk in all His ways, to obey His commands, to hold fast to Him and to serve Him with all your heart and all your soul."

Joshua 22:5

THE KEYS TO OBEDIENCE

God wants you to obey Him and walk closely with Him. Here are the keys to obedience:

- Love God with all your heart
- Honor your father and mother
- Be kind to others
- Act as Jesus would
- Speak the Truth
- Pray to God
- Go to church
- Read the Bible.

OPENING THE DOORS

The keys open God's doors to God's blessings in your life.

GOD

Healing	Patience
Wholeness	Kindness
Love	Self-control
Peace	Faithful
Joy	Gentleness

PUT ON THE WHOLE ARMOR OF GOD
Ephesians 6:10-18

1. **The Helmet of Salvation**
   I am your child. I am saved.

2. **The Breastplate of Righteousness**
   Have I done anything wrong?

3. **The Belt of Truth**
   I speak only Truth.

4. **The Shoes of the Gospel of Peace**
   Is there anyone I have not forgiven?

5. **The Shield of Faith**
   I trust Jesus at all times.

6. **The Sword of the Spirit.**
   The Bible speaks Truths to me.

7. **Pray in the Spirit**
   I praise and worship him daily.

In the name of Jesus, I put on the whole armor of God. I ask God to protect me from the lies and darts of the enemy which come against my body, soul, and spirit. Thank you, Lord. Amen

PRAYER OF AGREEMENT

God, once again I thank you for setting me free from all generational curses. You have removed them from my life. I thank you for sending your angels to watch over me at all times.

I ask the Holy Spirit to comfort and guide me and to lead me into the plan you have for my life. I will read your Word and try to do what is right. I will keep my body pure. I want to grow closer to you, and to serve you. I love you. Amen.

Date: _____   _____
                                 (Sign your name.)

                                 <u>Jesus Christ</u>
                          God, Jesus Christ, Holy Spirit

WATER BAPTISM

In Acts 22:16, it states *"And now what are you waiting for? Get up, be baptized and wash your sins away, calling on his name."*

It is clear that water baptism after believing in Jesus is a **commandment**. In Acts 16:30-33, it states, *"that as soon as they believed, they were baptized."* As soon as you believe in Jesus and repent, you are to be baptized.

The word baptism in the New Testament is bap-tid-zo and bap-tis-mos. These words mean fully wet; technique of the ordinance of Christ; to wash away; to immerse or dip under water. Jesus was baptized fully wet. The disciples were baptized fully wet. In baptism, we are identifying with Christ's death and resurrection.

Matthew 28:19-20 *Therefore, go and make disciples of all nations, baptizing them in the name of the Father and of the Son and of the Holy Spirit...*

HOLY SPIRIT BAPTISM

Acts 2:17-18 *In the last days, God says, I will pour out my Spirit on all people. Your sons and daughters will prophesy, your young men will see visions, your old men will dream dreams. Even on my servants, both men and women, I will pour out my Spirit in those days; and they will prophesy.*

What is the purpose of the Baptism of the Holy Spirit? Giving thanks, worshipping, and empowerment for service.

Acts 1:8 *But you shall receive power when the Holy Spirit comes on you; and you will be my witnesses in Jerusalem, and in all Judea and Samaria and to the end of the earth.*

Matthew 28:19 *Therefore go and make disciples of all nations, baptizing them in the name of the Father and of the Son and of the Holy Spirit.*

The Lord **commanded** us to receive the baptism of the Holy Spirit.

How do I receive the baptism of the Holy Spirit?

You receive this baptism by simply asking God for it.

The following is a prayer to receive the baptism of the Holy Spirit:

Lord Jesus, I thank you for dying on the cross for my sins and for being my Lord and Savior. I ask you to baptism me with your Holy Spirit. I ask you to empower me to be of service and to have the gift of speaking to you in other tongues. Thank you, Lord. Amen.

Do not be discouraged if the language does not come immediately. It may come while you are in the shower or riding in your automobile. Just continue to praise our Lord Jesus Christ, and you will begin to see change in your life.

SPIRITUALLY CLEAN YOUR ROOM

Pour a small amount of olive oil or cooking oil into a bowl and ask God to bless the oil.

In your room, dip your finger in the oil and put a cross on the doors and windows. (Include your closet door too.)

Pray and say out loud,

"If there is anything in my room that is not of God, then leave my room now in the name of Jesus Christ. You are not welcome here, and you are never to return.

Dear Lord, please bless my room and fill it with your Holy Spirit. Amen."

Only clean your room with oil once or when you sense it is spiritually unclean. At other times, just demand that anything that is not of God to leave your room. I usually do this at bed time.

CLOTHING WITH OCCULT SIGNS AND SYMBOLS

DO NOT REPRESENT THE ENEMY!

"Black Skull Sleeveless T-Shirt Iron Fist" "This black sleeveless T-shirt features a distressed pale blue front screen of skulls, lightning bolts and various phrases like 'Children of the night' and 'Fight back while you still can.'"(Internet Description)

This opposes the word of God who calls us children of light. The statement, "Fight back while you still can," is Satan admitting he has already been defeated. Jesus said, *"Take heart! I have overcome the world."* John 16:33

"Morbid Skull T-Shirt" "You ain't messin around with this shirt that says morbid all over front and back and has a sick bleach print of a skull with a dagger on its forehead." (Internet Description)"

The definition of morbid is unhealthy, diseased, and not wholesome. Jesus said of Satan, *"The thief comes only to steal and kill and destroy; I have come that they may have life, and have it to the full."* John 10:10

"World of War Craft™ Warlock Wow!" "Cast dark magic spells on all who cross you with this black T-shirt featuring a front screen of purple skulls and demons with a white Warlock hand logo." (Internet Description)"

"The power of God far exceeds the power of spells." Exodus 7:10-12

JEWELRY WITH OCCULT SIGNS AND SYMBOLS

Ankn Pendant

Bat Wing Skull Pendant

Cobra Head Pendant

Eagle's Wing Skull Pendant

Egyptian Symbol Necklace

Goddess Jewelry

Heartagram Pendant   Skull Pendant

 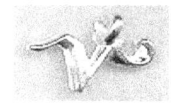

Zodiac Pendants

MEMORY VERSES

"...Love the Lord your God with all your heart and with all your soul and with all your mind."

Matthew 22:37

"Love your neighbor as yourself."

Matthew 22:39

"...I am the Lord, who heals you."

Exodus 15:26

GLOSSARY

Strongmen	Definition
Divination	fortune teller, magic
Familiar Spirit	drugs, yoga
Bondage	fears, addictions, wrong behaviors
Jealousy	anger, cruelty, jealousy, hatred
Lying Spirit	gossip, lies
Perverse Spirit	child abuse, evil actions
Pride	rebellion, prideful, arrogant, strife obstinate

Heaviness	sorrow, rejection, inner hurts
Whoredoms	love of money, eat too much,
Infirmity	sickness, disease
Dumb and Deaf	ear problems, mute, blindness, seizures
Fear	torment, bad dreams, doubt, fears
Seducing	deception, attraction to evil ways, lies
Anti-Christ	denies Christ
Error	unsubmissive, defensive, new age
Death	deception, lies

KEEPING YOUR CHILDREN SPIRITUALLY SAFE

Suggestions:

1. Pray protection, guidance, and for God's destiny for your children.

2. Spiritually cleanse their room on a regular basis.

3. Play Christian music in their room while sleeping (at a very low level).

4. Control what they watch on television.

   Do not let them watch anything that will cause fear or is violent.

5. Games such as Dungeons and Dragons are occult activities.

6. Scrutinize what they read. Materials that appear innocent often are not. The New Age theology seems to creep into reading

materials in a disguised form. Be on the alert!

7. Be aware of your children's friends.

8. Keep your children in a spirit-filled, bible-based church and involved in activities

REFERENCE BOOKS

Set Yourself Free Little Children and Come to Me is composed of original material and material from several other sources. We believe that all the materials are divinely inspired.

Reference material:

Kathryn Kuhlman's Healing Words, Library of Ralph Wilkerson (Creation House, Orlando, FL 1997) Page 4 – Prayer of Salvation

Dr. Carol Robeson, ***Strongman's His Name…What's His Game?*** (Shiloh Publishing House, Keizer, OR 1983, 1996)

Graphics by Microsoft Corp.

OTHER BOOKS BY LITTLE SPARROW MINISTRIES

Setting Yourself Free, Deliverance from Darkness (Little Sparrow Ministries, Copyright © 2001, 2003, 2008, 2013, 2017 Lindale, Texas 75771)

Targeted Prayers (Little Sparrow Ministries, Copyright © 2005, 2008, 2011, 2017 Lindale, Texas 75771)

Set Yourself Free Little Children and Come to Me (Little Sparrow Ministries, Copyright © 2001, 2003, 2017 Lindale, Texas 75771)

Truth vs. Lies, Information for Teenagers (Little Sparrow Ministries, Copyright © 2002, 2008, 2017 Lindale, Texas 75771)

Little Bit, the Miracle Kid (Little Sparrow Ministries, Copyright © 2009 Lindale, Texas 75771)

Have Faith, Inspirational Testimonies (Little Sparrow Ministries, Copyright © 2011 Lindale, Texas 75771)

I Am Abused (Little Sparrow Ministries, Copyright © 2017 Lindale, Texas 75771)

Collection of Letters from the Father's Heart (Little Sparrow Ministries, Copyright © 2017 Lindale, Texas 75771)

Freedom (Little Sparrow Ministries, Copyright © 2017 Lindale, Texas 75771)

He is in the Middle of Your Fire, Spiritual Workbook for PTSD (Little Sparrow Ministries, Copyright © 2017 Lindale, Texas 75771)

www.ingramcontent.com/pod-product-compliance
Lightning Source LLC
LaVergne TN
LVHW021741060526
838200LV00052B/3404